HERITAGE CLASSICS

Dr. Pawan Pokhariyal

ICU

ICU-1 AND ICU-2
(plays on the management of a patient of stroke in the ICU)

HERITAGE

HERITAGE PUBLISHERS
NEW DELHI

HERITAGE PUBLISHERS
19-A, Ansari Road, Daryaganj, New Delhi-110002
Tel.: 23266258, 23264444
Fax: 23263050, E-mail: info@heritagepublishers.in

ISBN : 978-817026-265-7

Printed in India
Sagar Printers, 23 Ansari Road
New Delhi-110002

Authors Note

This is the second set of two plays after "Tenants and Handshake "

Both the plays present management of a patient of stroke in an ICU. The plays also contains stories about two different families .

ICU-1

This is the story of a school teacher Mr. Gonzalez and his family. Mr. Gonzalez suffers from a stroke and is taken to an ICU after the critical period of 3 hrs.The main aim of the play is to present the treatment options available and the importance of prompt and immediate treatment .

ICU-2

The play ICU –2 presents the treatment of a patient of stroke who reaches the hospital within the critical period of 3 hrs.

This short skit is about Mr. Rakesh and his family who are staying in a rented house and are wanting to purchase a house when the incident happens ....

Only relevant medical facts are presented without going into details . The plays are not medical texts and only attempts to present relevant medical facts and information about the management of stroke to a non medical person. The language used to describe medical facts is also simplified to suit the requirements and understanding of a non-medical person.

ICU-1

(A play on the management of a patient of stroke in the ICU)

ICU - 1

The play presents the Condition, diagnosis, and treatment of a patient of stroke. The play shall consist of six acts, each act presenting an aspect pertaining to the management of the patient.

Characters

Mr. Robert Gonzalez: A middle aged teacher in a school nearby. Was earlier working in a college as a Professor. Later took up the job of a teacher in a school in which Simmy was studying in 1st grade. Looks like a scholar. Remains busy with his grandchildren at his house.

Mrs. Annie Gonzalez: Wife of Mr. Gonzalez. Wears glasses. Caring and loving. Was working as a primary school teacher previously.

Michael: Son of Mr. and Mrs. Gonzalez. An intelligent looking young man with all the ambitions of the youth.

Elizabeth: Wife of Michael. A beautiful and mature woman.

Simmy: 5 years old daughter of Michael and Elizabeth, cute and innocent.

John: 1year and 2 months old son of Michael and Elizabeth. Learning to walk and talk properly.

Dr Prakash: A neurologist at a reputed City hospital. A professional with a scientific look towards life.

Dr Diya: cardiologist at the same hospital.

Dr Grover: Neurosurgeon at the City hospital.

Dr. D'souza: An anaesthetist at city Hospital

Dr Sudheer: A duty doctor at the ICU. Hardworking and sincere.

Preparing for his Post-graduation exams.

A nurse at each bed of the ICU.

ICU

Scene of action

ACT –1: Mr. Gonzalez is playing with his grandchildren at his home. The act takes place in the entrance hall of Mr. Gonzalez's residence.

ACT– 2: The scene takes place in the room of Mr. and Mrs. Gonzalez.

A simple room with two beds, a table and a chair.

ACT-3: 12 bedded ICU in a metropolitan city hospital equipped with state of art medical facilities including ventilators, pulse and BP monitors. The ICU kept neat and tidy.

A nurse at each bed. Many doctors at work.

ACT 4: Takes place in the same ICU mentioned above.

ACT 5: Takes place in a hospital ward. Simple and clean room with a bed for the patient and nurse in the room for giving medicines.

ACT –6 Takes place at the entrance hall at Dr Diya's residence. Well furnished and decorated.

ACT 1

The house of Mr. Gonzalez is simple. A gate at the entrance on the left side opens into a pathway. A small parking space straight ahead. A garden on the right side and front. A few steps before the parking space take us to the verandah where a few chairs are kept around a round table. A door opens into the reception hall which is simple and beautifully decorated.

Two bedrooms on right side of the reception hall with bathroom and toilets. The reception hall has sofas around a round table. A television near the sofas. Still ahead is a small dining table and chairs. A kitchen door near the dining table.

Mr. Gonzalez is teaching John to walk in the reception hall. He is holding John's hand and asking him to take steps. Mrs. Gonzalez is knitting a sweater for John.

Simmy is seated on the sofa.

Mr. Gonzalez: Dear John take one step ahead. Slowly then next.

John: Grandpa..grandpa ...... *(takes few steps ahead.)*

Mr. Gonzalez: Good. You shall be able to walk Properly in few days.

Annie look John has started to walk a bit.

Mrs. Gonzalez: Good John.

Simmy: Dear grandma, I want something to eat.

Mrs. Gonzalez:Simmy wait, I shall prepare noodles for both of you.

Mrs. Gonzalez goes to the kitchen.

Mr. Gonzalez: John must learn walking by next month.

Simmy: Grandpa put on the TV. My cartoon show is about to start.

Mr. Gonzalez: Ok dear hold your brother. *(Simmy holds her brother)*

Grandpa puts on the TV.

Simmy: Grandpa get me noodles.

Mr. Gonzalez: Simmy noodles are getting ready.

Mrs. Gonzalez *(from the kitchen)*: Noodles are getting prepared Simmy. Wait a while.

Mr. Gonzalez: Have you completed your homework, Simmy?

Simmy: Yes grandpa.

Mr. Gonzalez: Show me your homework when the cartoon show is over.

Simmy: Yes, grandpa. Oh! My cartoon show has started.

John: Cartoon,..........cartoon

Mr. Gonzalez: Okay John the walking practice shall resume soon after the cartoons.

(Mr. Gonzalez takes John to the sofa and watches the cartoon along with Simmy) Mrs. Gonzalez brings a bowl of noodles and few plates from kitchen. She puts the noodles on the table and serves noodles in plates.

Mrs. Gonzalez: Come Simmy take your plate of

noodles. Robert take this plate for John.

Mr. Gonzalez feeds noodles to John. Simmy takes her plate.

John: Noodles, noodles..

Mrs. Gonzalez: Next week, the children want to go to some hilly region for summer vacation.

Mr. Gonzalez: That's nice.

Mrs. Gonzalez: They were asking if we both would like to come as well.

Mr. Gonzalez: Let the children enjoy.We both shall stay at our home.

Mrs. Gonzalez: John and Simmy shall also go with them. They shall be away for ten days.

Mr. Gonzalez: I would like John to start walking properly before they go to any hill station. When are they planning their trip?

Mrs. Gonzalez: Next month beginning.

Mr. Gonzalez: Two weeks from now. In another two weeks John shall be walking on his own.

Simmy: Grandma, I want more noodles.

Mrs. Gonzalez: Simmy give me your plate.

(brings some more noodles for Simmy)

Simmy: The cartoon show is over. Grandpa tell us a story.

Mr. Gonzalez: Simmy Grandpa is having slight headache. I shall tell you a story some other day.

Simmy: Story, grandpa.

Mrs. Gonzalez: *(brings some tablets with water)*Take these tablets for your headache.*(Mr. Gonzalez takes the tablets)*

John: Story.........

Mr. Gonzalez: Little John also wants to hear a story. Ok I shall tell you a short story from my school days.

Trekking

Simmy do you know that we have NCC (National cadet corps) training course in the school. You must have seen young scouts and guides in the school. We too had similar NCC training during our school days. I too joined NCC during my school years. The NCC training arranged trekking to various picnic sites nearby. The NCC organized trekking every 3 months. A group of students would first search for a picnic site usually near a riverside. The students would leave along the route many NCC trekking signs. The second group of students would search for the picnic spot by tracing the trekking signs. Once both the groups had found each other, a camp would be setup near the riverside. The students would put tents, arrange for food, prepare song, dance and skits and would prepare for spending the entire day at the camp. The entire day was full of fun and enjoyment. The trekking was organized by a trekking guide who was a senior scout.

During one of the trekking trips a camp was setup near a riverside. After setting their tents the students had some snacks. The students who were good swimmers started swimming. Do you know that I too was a good swimmer of the class?

Simmy: Yes. You have told us about your swimming

capabilities many a times to us. Grandpa continue the story.

Mr. Gonzalez: *(holds his head with headache)* Simmy I shall tell you the story some other day.

Simmy: Grandpa, you don't seem to be well. Tell the story some other day.

Mrs. Gonzalez: Robert are you all right?

Mr. Gonzalez: I am all right Annie. I shall finish the story fast and take some rest.

A classmate Rajender was learning to swim. The students used to bring rubber tubes to learn swimming. He took a similar rubber tube and started practising to swim. Those who were learning were advised not to go to the deeper water. It so happened that the rubber tube in which Rajender was practising to swim suddenly slipped out of his hands and Rajender started shouting and struggling in the water. All the swimmers rushed towards Rajender and gripped his legs and started dragging him to the riverbank. Other cadets also joined and Rajender was taken to the corner.

His abdomen was squeezed to bring out water from abdomen and chest. Rajender soon recovered and thanked everyone for the rescue. The rest of the trekking the cadets spent enjoying their lunch and the scenery. The cadets returned to their homes in the evening.

Simmy: Even I would join NCC when I grow up.

Mr. Gonzalez: Good.

Dear Simmy, grandpa is having slight

headache. He shall tell you a nice story some other day.

Mrs. Gonzalez: Are you taking your BP and sugar tablets regularly?

Mr. Gonzalez: Yes, of course.

Mrs. Gonzalez: You have not been taking your BP medicines properly. Have you renewed your medical insurance?

Mr. Gonzalez: Yes. I did so while returning from the school.

Mrs. Gonzalez: Good.

Simmy: Grandma,you make very good noodles.

Grandma smiles.

Mr. Gonzalez: Of course she cooks well. Earlier she used to cook dishes of my liking as well. These days she only prepares dishes which the children like.

Mrs. Gonzalez: You have started behaving like a child again. Just yesterday I made the vegetable soup of your liking.

Grandpa: Ok.

The doorbell rings.

Mrs. Gonzalez opens the door. Michael and Elizabeth enter into the room.

Michael takes both children in his arms and hugs them.

Elizabeth: Did they behave properly?

Mrs. Gonzalez: Yes, they did.

Elizabeth hugs the children as well.

Elizabeth: Simmy, show me your homework after

you finish eating your noodles.

Michael: Mother what have you decided about coming to the hill station?

Mrs. Gonzalez: We have seen the place many a times. We shall stay at home. In fact myself and your grandpa met each other for the first time at the same hill station when we were still in our colleges. Our families were well known to each other and they were expecting us to get married. (the children listen intently)

Elizabeth: Mother even if you have seen the place we are visiting, you are welcome to come with us. Michael shall bring two more tickets.Think again and tell us in a few days.

Michael: Mr. Seth has invited us all for a dinner on the occassion of their 5 yr old son's birthday They have asked us to invite both of you as well. Would you like to come?

Mrs. Gonzalez: Your father is having headache since afternoon. He took some medicines few minutes back. It will be better if both of us stay at home tonight.

Michael: All Right.We shall be back home early and shall bring something for both of you. Show yourself to some doctor coming morning.

Elizabeth: Simmy show your homework.

Simmy: Ok.

Simmy brings some notebooks and shows the homework to her mother.

John: Grandma ....noodles ....noodles.

Mrs. Gonzalez feeds noodles to john.

Elizabeth: The homework seems to be all right.

Simmy you can come for the party tonight.

A phone bell rings. Elizabeth picks up the phone. She reads the message sent.

Elizabeth: Mother get the children ready. Mr. Seth has sent a message. Simmy get ready for the party.

Simmy: Ok mother.

Mrs. Gonzalez: Come Simmy. I shall get both of you ready for the party.

Michael and Elizabeth go to their room, Mrs. Gonzalez takes John and Simmy to their rooms holding John in her arms. Mr. Gonzalez puts on a different channel on the TV and leans over the sofa. He is often seen holding and massaging his head. Elizabeth is seen going to the kitchen. She prepares few sandwiches for Mr. & Mrs. Gonzalez, then she goes to her room to prepare herself for the party.

Soon the Michael family reenters the room fully prepared for the party.

Elizabeth is holding John in her arms.

Elizabeth: John you must learn walking soon.

John: Grandpa, ...,walking.

Elizabeth: Mother, Father take your noodles properly. I have prepared some sandwiches for both of you. We shall return as early as possible.

Mrs. Gonzalez: Don't worry about us dear. Enjoy your party.

Michael's family leaves for the party. John is heard.

John: Grand ma .....Grandpa.

Mr. Gonzalez: Without the grandchildren the house... seems deserted.

Mrs. Gonzalez: They shall return soon.Watch your program me till then. I shall bring some sandwiches and noodles for both of us. Let the children spend a good evening together.

Mrs. Gonzalez brings two plates full of noodles and a plate of sandwiches. She puts the dishes on the table and serves sandwiches and noodles to Mr. Gonzalez on a plate.

Both talk to each other while eating their dinner.

Mr. Gonzalez: Its been days since we spent the time together like this. Michael and his family are visiting the same place where we had met the first time.We can talk of our old days....

When we got married and the day we shifted to this house....The day when Michael was born... The day Michael got married....

The day John and Simmy were born....

And about all the events which have made the life interesting.

Mrs. Gonzalez: Tell me a week when you haven't talked about the same events since past 32 years of marriage.

Mr. Gonzalez: The days seem to pass so fast with our grandchildren. Till they return, come let us watch a movie together.

Mrs. Gonzalez: Eat your dinner first. How is your headache?

Mr. Gonzalez: Better.

Mrs. Gonzalez: Tomorrow we shall go to the family physician.

Mr. Gonzalez: Okay.

They watch a movie together ,singing songs and eating noodles and sandwiches.

Mr. Gonzalez: Annie do you remember our first meeting at the same hill station where Michael and his family are going to visit.We met at a party. Our families were known to each other and all of them were expecting us to get married.

Mrs. Gonzalez: Yes of course. I still remember the day, we were too young and shy.

(and they are taken into the nostalgic lanes of the past)

Annie an Robert at the party

(The Heart and the Brain)

Annie and Robert had come to attend a party with their families. Their families had known each other since a long time. They lived together in a village. Robert's family later shifted to a city. The party was arranged for introducing Annie and Robert to each other.

Robert: If I am not wrong, you are Annie, my childhood friend.

Annie: Yes I am the same Annie.You are Robert.

Robert: You still Haven't forgotten your childhood friend.

Annie: How can I forget someone with whom I spent most of my childhood. Played and grew together before you went to the city and I stayed at the same village.

Robert: And how beautiful you have grown over the years.

Annie: You too have grown into a fine and handsome man.

Robert: Everyone at the party are looking at us. If you listen to their whispers, they are talking of how beautiful a pair we both make.

Annie: And what do you feel yourself Robert?

Robert: Dear Annie, you look exactly like the woman of my dreams. We do make a wonderful pair.

Annie: Our parents have got us together expecting both of us to like each other and get married. Do you have any other intensions?

Robert: Dear Annie marriage is definitely an option. Before marriage it is essential that we know about each other.

Annie: Dear Robert we have been good friends before, I feel we would soon learn to understand each other well.

Robert: Dear Annie you grew up in a village. On the other hand our family grew up in a city. The city life is real fast. Would you make adjustments if necessary? I think we should take some time before taking a final decision.

Annie: Dear Robert, we would learn to adjust once we know more of each other.

Robert: Definitely.

Annie: Robert did you remember me all these years?

Robert: Yes of course.

Annie: Good. We Can expect a good relationship. What else are you interested in?

Robert: Science ,philosophy ,art and architecture. What about you?

Annie: I am interested in music ,poetry and dance. Robert we differ so much.

Annie: We would have to search for something which is common in us. We shall learn gradually to complement each other.

Robert: Why not? Let us begin to love each other.

Annie: Dear Robert you will have to be more romantic with me..

Robert: You are right.But you see I have no experiences in the matter of the heart. You will have to tell me about love. I regard love only as an idea.

Annie: You should understand that ideas are not sufficient. You also require experiences to know what the ideas mean.

Robert: You seem to be correct. If we discuss about life and learn to live perfectly we would definitely learn more about love and also about other ideas which are progressive and help us evolve.

Annie: We could learn of the ideas by gradually experiencing life.

Robert: True. We can definitely try out marriage.

Annie: You must learn about how to propose first.

Robert: How do you expect me to do so when I have not done anything like that before.

Annie: Ok.First say I love you.

Robert: Let us both do it together.

Robert and Annie: I Love you.

Annie: Well a good beginning.

Robert: What do you do Annie?

Annie: I am doing a course to become a teacher.

Robert: I am doing a course of advanced mathematics.

Annie: Impressive.Everyone is looking at us.

Annie: Lets convey our intentions to everyone.

Robert: Ok.

Robert and Annie return to the party and tell their parents about agreeing to marry.

Annie and Robert return back to their room from their memories.

Annie: Do you remember the letters which we sent to each other.

Robert: Yes.

Annie: I'll get some of them from the suitcase.

Annie gets few letters from her room. She reads important portions of the letters which she had marked with a pen.

Dear Annie

Hello, how are you? I am about to complete my course. I shall soon be self—sufficient. We both would be full-fledged professionals and could think of putting our education to work. Hope you too must be completing your education soon.

We had agreed to keep communicating so send a reply. I am sending you few lines of a poem. I shall read the entire poem to you when we

meet again.
Miles apart
still I could hear the beating of your heart.
Still in memories,
Those discussions on philosophy and science
Giving a mature touch to our drives.

With best wishes
Robert

Annie sends a reply.

Hello, Dear Robert,

received your letter. Good that you are completing your course.I too shall be completing my education in few months. Acquired lot of skills during final year of training. I shall tell you more when we meet each other. Sending a poem to maintain communication. I penned these lines while thinking about love and you.

LOVE

So subtle
Defies hence all definitions
Makes the body aware
Of the existence of the self and others
Bridging all the dissimilarity
Striving ever to achieve uniformity
Just solve the inner mystery
And thou become aware of the idea
And its universality.
More profound than the components microscopic

And more universal than the bodies celestial.
It resides here in every heart
Circulates through every part.
Assemble
Lets achieve a synthesis
Let every heart speak a story unique
Of a rejuvenation in the language of love.

With love
Annie

A few days later she receives a reply.

Hello, Dear Annie,

received your reply. I have completed my course and have received my degree. You sent me a nice poem about Love. Its nice to know that you have such views about love.Read the lines of a poem below and tell me whether my views about love are correct or not. I shall show you the entire poem on returning home.

Passions when translate themselves into poetry
Feelings for the beloved when become a symphony
When instincts transform into absolute creativity
Love thenceforth rises to its true ability.

I shall be coming to see you soon.

Yours only
Robert

Annie receives the letter and replies.

Your views about love were nice. I feel that passions and feelings are also important. They provide the necessary experience. Without experiences life becomes less interesting. I hope you would understand. Hope to see you soon. We shall discuss more about love, as soon as you reach here.

With Love

Annie.

Both Annie and Robert complete their courses in honors and put their knowledge and skills to proper work in the service of humanity and life.

(Annie and Robert return to their home from their past)

Both remain awake till Michael and Elizabeth return home with John and Simmy.

John is sleeping in Elizabeth's arms. She takes him to his room.

Michael: Father, Mother, you are still awake?

Elizabeth returns to the entrance room.

Elizabeth: Did you eat your sandwiches and noodles?

Mrs. Gonzalez: Yes we did. How was your party?

Elizabeth: The children did not allow us to stay in the party. Simmy kept asking about both of you. John was also sleeping so we returned as quickly as possible.

Mr. Gonzalez: Take Simmy to her room as well.

Simmy: Grandpa, story...story.

Michael: No story Simmy. Let grandpa rest. Come to your room.

Elizabeth and Michael take Simmy to their room.

Mrs. Gonzalez: Have you taken your BP and sugar tablets. I haven't seen you taking your tablets properly these days.

Mr. Gonzalez: I shall take the tablets before sleeping.

Mrs. Gonzalez and Mr. Gonzalez go to their room.

ACT 2

The room of Mr. Gonzalez is simple. Two beds on one side. An almirah, a table and a chair on other side. Mr. and Mrs. Gonzalez on the beds sleeping.

Mr. Gonzalez gets up at night at around 2 am. Tries to get up from the bed but finds it difficult to get up. Takes a tablet kept on the bed. He notices slight numbness on left arm while taking the tablet.

Mr. Gonzalez: Must be the arthritis again.

He sleeps again.

In the morning.

Mrs.Gonzalez: How long will you keep sleeping. Get up from bed.

(Removes the curtains)

Mr. Gonzalez: The headache… kept bothering me the entire night. I had… to take a tablet. My left arm was moving less. I thought it was arthritis. *(Tries to get up from the bed, the left arm doesn't move properly.)*

Mrs. Gonzalez: Don't be lazy.Get up from the bed. *(Supports Mr. Gonzalez)*

Mr. Gonzalez tries again but in vain.

Mrs.Gonzalez: What happened to you? *(Mrs. Gonzalez cries out)*: Michael... Elizabeth… come soon...

Michael enters the room.

Mrs. Gonzalez: Look Michael... Doctor, call the doctor.

Michael: What happened mother?

Mrs. Gonzalez: Robert is not moving his left arm properly. He is having headache. Call the doctor.

Michael looks at Mr. Gonzalez. Mr. Gonzalez tries to get up again.

(Mr. Gonzalez gradually becomes drowsy)

Michael calls up a doctor...

Michael: Hello doctor Diwakar. Father is having difficulty to get up from bed. He is not moving his left arm properly. He had slight headache yesterday night. ...Okay Doctor ...come soon doctor.

(to his mother)

I have called doctor Diwakar.He shall be here soon.

Mrs. Gonzalez: Bring some headache tablets.

Michael: Let Dr Diwakar come.

(*Elizabeth enters the room.*)

Elizabeth: What happened?

Michael: Father is not well. We have called Dr Diwakar. He shall be here soon.

Elizabeth holds Mrs. Gonzalez's hands and tries to console and support her.

Mrs. Gonzalez: Get some water for your father.

Elizabeth: Okay.

Simmy enters the room.

Simmy: What happened grandma?

Mrs. Gonzalez: Everything is fine dear. You are not ready for your school. Take Simmy along with you Elizabeth and prepare her for the school.

(Elizabeth takes Simmy to her room.

The doorbell rings, Dr Diwakar enters the room.)

Dr Diwakar: Mr. Gonzalez, How are you?

Mr. Gonzalez: Hm.mmmm headache.

Mrs.Gonzalez: He had slight headache yesterday night. He took some tablets and slept. He says he got up in the night and took one more headache tablet. In the morning he couldn't get up from his bed properly. He is moving his left arm lesser than right.

Dr Diwakar: Was he taking his BP and sugar medicines properly?

Mrs. Gonzalez: No, he was taking them irregularly.

Dr Diwakar: Did he take the medicines yesterday night.

Mrs. Gonzalez: I didn't see him taking.

Dr Diwakar examines Mr. Gonzalez. Takes his BP.

Dr Diwakar: Since when did you notice the weakness on the left arm?

Mr. Gonzalez: *(with slight difficulty)* Yester..day….. I.. Got up at around……. 2 am …...and noticed ….my arm was numb. …...had difficulty getting up from bed.

Dr Diwakar: He must be shifted to a hospital immediately. He should have been shifted to a hospital yesterday night itself.

Michael: Is there anything serious doctor?

Dr Diwakar: It seems like a stroke.These days there are medicines to treat a stroke if the patient reports in time. We must shift him immediately.

(Dr Diwakar gives an injection and some tablets to Mr. Gonzalez. Elizabeth brings some water and helps Mr. Gonzalez take the tablets)

Dr Diwakar: I have given him an injection for the headache and some medicines. I will call the ambulance.

(Calls up an emergency ambulance service)

Hello....yes...we require an ambulance urgently with all the emergency facilities. Okay......note the address *(reads the address of Mr. Gonzalez)*....The ambulance shall be here any moment. Prepare Mr. Gonzalez for shifting to a hospital.

Mrs. Gonzalez: *(prepares Mr. Gonzalez)* Do I need to take anything along doctor?

Dr. Diwakar: No Mrs. Gonzalez just give him a mouth wash and comb his hairs.It shall be enough. Take his old medical records along.

Mrs. Gonzalez: Okay.*(She does the same and takes some medical papers from the almirah)*

Soon an ambulance horn is heard outside.Two ward boys enter the room with a stretcher.

Ward boy: Where is the patient?

Dr. Diwakar: Mr. Gonzalez, wake up, we are taking you to the hospital. *(tries to wake up Mr. Gonzalez)* Shift him to the ambulance.

The ward boys shift Mr. Gonzalez on the stretcher and take him to the ambulance.Michael goes along with the stretcher.

Mrs. Gonzalez: Elizabeth , I am going with Michael to the hospital, stay with Simmy and John. Send Simmy to her school. If you come to hospital do not bring John.

Elizabeth: Ok. I shall ask my sister to look after him.

Simmy enters the room.

Simmy: Grandma, is grand pa all right? I saw him taken to an ambulance in a stretcher.

Mrs.Gonzalez: Grandpa is going to a hospital for medical check up. He shall return home soon.

Simmy: I also want to come to the hospital.

Mrs.Gonzalez: Simmy you prepare to go to school. You have to show your homework to the teacher. Elizabeth drop her to the school.

Elizabeth: Don't worry mother. I shall take her to school. Come Simmy get ready for the school.

Michael is heard from outside the house.

Michael: Mother come soon.

Mrs. Gonzalez leaves the room.

Elizabeth takes away Simmy to her room.

ACT 3 Part I

At the hospital, inside the ICU, a resident Doctor is taking the clinical history. Mr. Gonzalez is lying on a bed. Few IV lines and IV fluids on flow. A nurse is busy giving medicines. Mrs. Gonzalez and Michael are seated on two chairs in front of the resident doctor's *(Dr Sudheer)* table and chair. Dr Sudheer is a young, active and experienced doctor.

He introduces himself and asks Mrs. Gonzalez and Michael their names, then

Resident: Mrs. Gonzalez and Mr. Michael give me details about what happened?

Mrs. Gonzalez: He had slight headache in the afternoon yesterday. He kept taking headache tablets every 6 hours. He says he got up at around 2 am last night and was unable to get up from bed properly. Had numbness of the left arm. He took another tablet kept near the bed and slept till 9 am. I had to wake him up. Was not moving his left arm properly. We called our family doctor who advised us to shift him to a hospital immediately. He had an episode of vomiting before coming to the hospital.

Resident: Did he have any fits?

Mrs. Gonzalez: No.

Resident: Does he have Sugar or BP?

Mrs. Gonzalez: He has both BP and sugar since 4 years. He tried to control BP and sugar with diet control for 2 years. Then Dr Diwakar started him on medicines for both. He is on those medicines since then.

Resident: Can you show me the medicines or the prescriptions?

Michael: Here are Dr Diwakar prescriptions.

Resident: Does he take any other medicines?

Mrs. Gonzalez: No

Resident: Anything more you wish to tell or ask.

Michael: Dr Diwakar was telling us about some medicine which could improve Mr. Gonzalez's condition.

Resident: The medicine is given when the patient has a stroke and arrives within 3 hours to the hospital. Mr. Gonzalez had weakness of left hand at 2 am. Its already more than 3 hours. Let Dr. Prakash who is a consultant Neurologist come.He shall tell you more about Mr. Gonzalez's condition and treatment.

Keep the medicines and old medical records of Mr. Gonzalez in the ICU for Dr Prakash to see. We'll have to do a CT scan of head and a MRI to confirm the diagnosis.

Michael takes out all the medical records of Mr. Gonzalez and keeps the records on the table for the resident's perusal. The resident reads the papers and relevant facts in the records.

Resident: Okay. Dr. Prakash shall be here any moment. He shall have a look at Mr. Gonzalez and shall talk to both of you. Meanwhile you both can take a room for yourself. Write down your phone number in the file so that we could call you up in any emergency.

(to the Nurse)

Sister note the phone numbers of the patient and his attenders.

Complete other formalities as well. Get me the treatment chart. I shall start the patient on some medicines. Dr Prakash shall be here soon and decide the rest of the treatment.

Michael writes the phone numbers and address on the file.

Michael: Doctor call us if there is any requirement. What if we wish to know about the patient?

Resident: You can call at ICU phone number whenever you wish to ask us anything. Dr Prakash shall call you to his room and tell you about the patient management. Thank you for giving all the details about the patient.

Mrs. Gonzalez and Michael leave ICU.

Dr Prakash (Neurologist) *enters the ICU along with two other doctors*

Dr Prakash: Where is the new patient Mr. Gonzalez?

Resident: On bed no. 6.

The resident takes Dr. Prakash to Mr. Gonzalez and presents the relevant medical history.

Resident: Mr. Gonzalez is 62 years old male, known case of Diabetes and Hypertension on regular treatment. Has presented with headache since yesterday afternoon. Took some headache tablets. Got up at 2 am in the morning and couldn't get up from bed. Had numbness in left arm. In the morning woke up at around 9 am and had weakness in left arm of the body. Was seen by the family physician and shifted to the hospital at around 9.30 am today for further management. On examination of the patient…

Dr Prakash: Dr Sudheer let me examine the patient on my own. Mr. Gonzalez I am Dr Prakash. How are you?

Mr. Gonzalez: ….Fine ….

Dr Prakash examines Mr. Gonzalez.

Dr. Prakash: Move your left arm Mr. Gonzalez.

Mr. Gonzalez: Ok. *(tries to move, left arm Dr Prakash notices the weakness)*

Dr Prakash: Show me the treatment chart. *(scribbles few drugs on the treatment chart)* Start these medicines. Get a CT scan of the head immediately. Get an MRI if CT doesn't suggest anything. I shall add few more drugs after the CT and MRI is done. Monitor BP and sugar.

Dr Prakash leaves the ICU.

Dr Sudheer: *(to the ward boy)* Shift the patient to the CT room.

The ward boy shifts the patient to the CT room on a trolley. Soon the trolley returns. Mr. Gonzalez is shifted to his ICU bed.The resident calls up Dr Prakash.

Resident: *(Calls over the phone)* Dr Prakash speaking. Yes We have got the CT as well as the MRI of Mr. Gonzalez.Yes ,yes I got the films to the ICU.

The resident examines Mr. Gonzalez again.

Soon Dr Prakash enters the ICU.

Examines CT and MRI films.

Dr Prakash: I am adding few drugs in the treatment chart. Call Mrs. Gonzalez and her son to the ICU.

Resident *(calls up)*: Send Mrs. Gonzalez and her Son to the ICU.

Dr Prakash takes a chair.

Soon Mrs. Gonzalez and Michael enter the ICU. Dr. Prakash introduces himself, then

Michael: Dr Prakash what does the CT and MRI report suggest?

Dr Prakash: A minor stroke.

The blood supply of a small portion of the brain has got obstructed which has damaged the area. We have started the treatment.

Mrs. Gonzalez: Doctor when is he going to recover? Dr Diwakar was telling me about some clot dissolving medicine?

Dr Prakash: Mrs. Gonzalez we have taken care of every aspect regarding patient management. We have added all necessary treatment for the patient. Since the weakness started at night we are not adding the clot dissolving medicine because three hours have already elapsed. If everything goes well he can be shifted to room in few days. He shall continue to require physiotherapy and few drugs. The recovery of weakness may require 1-2 months.

Michael: Doctor are there any complications?

Dr Prakash: We will have to keep patient under observation for next few days.Physiotherapy and exercises shall remain the main treatment with few drugs. The patient may develop swelling in the area of stroke, due to which patient may become drowsy. The area of stroke may increase causing increase in weakness. If patient shows any signs of deterioration, then we will have to take surgery opinion from Neurosurgeons.

Michael: Thank you doctor.

Dr Prakash: You can call the ICU doctor whenever you wish to enquire about the patient's condition. *(to the resident)* Call Dr Diya and get cardiology opinion and an ECHO done.

Mrs. Gonzalez goes to see Mr. Gonzalez: How are you?

Mr. Gonzalez: The headache has improved...

Mrs. Gonzalez: Get well soon. Simmy and John are missing you.

Mr. Gonzalez: hm...Okay..

Mrs. Gonzalez and Michael leave the ICU.

Dr Prakash:*(to the resident)* Keep a close watch over his condition.

Resident: Ok. There are new admissions in other wards.

Dr Prakash: Yes I have list of new admissions with me. I shall have a look at them on my own. You take care of the patients in this ward.

Dr Prakash leaves the ICU.

Resident Calls up Dr Diya: Dr Diya speaking?... Yes there is an ECHO to be done and cardiology opinion....The Patient's name is Mr. Gonzalez... Bed No. 6...Neurology ICU.

Soon Dr Diya enters the ICU with a technician and an echo cardiograph.

Dr Diya: Where is Mr. Gonzalez?

The resident takes Dr Diya to Mr. Gonzalez.

She reads the case file and looks at the ECG and performs ECHO of Mr. Gonzalez. She reads the old records of Mr. Gonzalez.

Dr Diya: The ECHO is normal. I shall talk to Dr. Prakash.Give me the attenders number as well.

The resident gives the numbers to Dr Diya.

Dr Diya leaves the ICU.

The resident examines Mr. Gonzalez, and other patients in the ICU. Instructs the sister to have a close watch.

ACT 3 Part-II

Three days later Michael visits the ICU in the morning.

Michael: Father. *(Mr. Gonzalez responds drowsily)*

Mr. Gonzalez: h..m...

Michael to the resident: Doctor Mr. Gonzalez looks very drowsy.

Resident: Yes, he is very drowsy since morning. We have got a CT scan done. The CT shows increase in swelling. I have talked to Dr Prakash about the patient condition. He shall be in the ICU soon.

Michael: Dr Prakash did tell us about swelling at the site of stroke.

Resident: Despite the medicines there has been an increase in the swelling.

Dr Prakash enters the ICU with two other Doctors. One of the doctors is Dr Grover, a neurosurgeon.

Dr Prakash: Show me the CT. *(Dr Prakash and Dr Grover study the CT)*

Dr. Prakash: The swelling has increased. Mr. Michael meet Dr. Grover. He is a neurosurgeon in the hospital. Dr. Grover what do you suggest?

Dr Grover: The patient shall require surgery if there is any further increase in the swelling. We'll have to keep a close watch over his condition. Presently he can be continued on medicines. Inform me about the patient's condition regularly. Give me consent papers. I shall write down the risk factors for the surgery. *(A nurse brings a consent paper, Dr. Grover writes down the risk factors for surgery and leaves the ICU with Dr. Prakash.)*

Resident to the nurse: Keep the patient on IV fluids.

Dr. D'souza *(An Anaesthetist)* enters the ICU.

Reads the file and sees all the investigations.

Dr. D'souza: *(Addresses Michael)* Hello, I am Dr. D'souza, an Anaesthetist. Iam examining the patient so that everything is ready for any emergency surgery. Are you with the patient?

Michael: Yes.

Dr. D'souza: I have already known much about the patient from the file. Did the patient have any allergy to any drug?

Michael: No.

Dr. D'souza: Does the patient have any artificial dentures?

Michael: No.

Dr. D'souza: Was he on any medication other than those mentioned in the file for BP and sugar?

Michael: No. Occasionally he used to take some ayurvedic tablets and vitamins.

Dr. D'souza: Okay that shall be fine. I have already seen the file and have known whatever is relevant. Thank you.

Dr. D'souza leaves the ICU. Michael also leaves after a while.

ACT 4
Section I

A study room for doctors in the hospital with few tables and chairs and cabinets with books.

Dr Sudheer is studying in the library.

Dr Prakash enters the room.

Dr Prakash: Dr Sudheer how are you?

Dr Sudheer: Fine.How are you sir?

Dr Prakash: Fine.How is your preparation for the post graduation proceeding?

Dr Sudheer: Well, still to study a lot.

Dr Prakash: How is Mr. Gonzalez?

Dr Sudheer: He is doing well.

Dr. Prakash: Seems like Mr. Gonzalez may not require surgery and recover with the medicines.

Dr. Sudheer: Yes he looked stable.

Dr Prakash: If the patient remains stable for another few days he can be shifted to the ward.

Dr. Sudheer: Yes.

Dr Prakash: How are his BP and sugar today.

Dr Sudheer: Within normal levels.

Dr Prakash: Ok. Had your lunch?

Dr Sudheer: Not yet. I shall have the lunch after I complete studying few chapters.

Dr Grover enters the room.

Dr Grover: How are you Dr Prakash?

Dr Prakash: Fine Dr Grover. How are you?

Dr Grover: Fine.

Dr Grover: How is your patient Mr. Gonzalez?

Dr Prakash: The patient is doing fine. In few days we are shifting him to the ward.

Dr Grover: Good that he didn't require surgery.

Dr Prakash: Yes.

Dr Grover: Medical science has developed so well in few years. Today we have so many treatment options for a patient of stroke. Apart from medicines,we have surgical options as well. Few years back there were not many options available.

Dr Prakash: Yes we indeed have many treatment option available these days.

Dr Grover: I heard from colleagues that a patient was given the new clot dissolving drug recently and his left arm weakness improved completely.

Dr Prakash: Yes a patient by the name of Mr. Rakesh was admitted with left arm weakness like Mr. Gonzalez. He was given the new drug and showed immediate improvement. He shall be shifted to the ward coming morning.

Dr Grover: So the drug is effective.

Dr Prakash:Yes.

Dr Grover: Sudheer are you preparing for post graduation.

Dr Sudheer: Yes sir.

Dr Grover:Take some notes from the postgraduates.

Dr Sudheer: Ok.

Dr Grover: Continue with your studies.

(takes a book from the shelf and starts reading)

After a while, Dr Sudheer gets up to go the ICU.

Dr Grover: Going to the ICU.

Dr. Sudheer: Yes.

Dr. Grover: Keep informing me about Mr. Gonzalez

Dr. Sudheer: Ok.

Dr. Grover and Dr Prakash: Good luck for the exams.

Dr. Sudheer: Thank You.

Dr. Sudheer leaves the study room with few books in his hand.

ACT 4
Section II

A Few days later...

Dr Sudheer enters the ICU and takes a short round examining each patient.

Dr Sudheer: *(to the nurse)* Sister call Mrs. Gonzalez.

Nurse: *(calls over the phone)* Hello Send Mrs. Gonzalez to the ICU. ....The doctor wishes to talk to the attendant.

Soon Mrs. Gonzalez arrives in the ICU.

Dr Sudheer: Hello, Mrs. Gonzalez. Please take a seat.

Mrs. Gonzalez: Thank you Doctor.

Dr Sudheer: Mrs. Gonzalez, I have good news to give you.Almost 2 weeks have passed since Mr. Gonzalez got admitted to the ICU. Today we are shifting the patient to room.

Mrs. Gonzalez: What doctor?

Dr Sudheer: Mr. Gonzalez shall be shifted to the ward at around 11 am.

Mrs. Gonzalez: *(Happily)* That's really a good news for us. Is Robert stable enough?

Dr Sudheer:Yes.

Mrs. Gonzalez: So Robert won't require surgery any more.

Dr Sudheer: No. His swelling is reduced and he has shown much improvement.

Mrs. Gonzalez: Thank you doctor.

Dr Sudheer: Arrange a room in the hospital so that we could shift him at the earliest.

Mrs. Gonzalez: Ok doctor, where should I go to arrange a room?

Dr Sudheer: Go to the administration section and meet Mr. Chaturvedi. He shall provide you a room according to your requirements.

Mrs. Gonzalez: Thank you doctor.

Mrs. Gonzalez leaves the ICU.

ACT 5
Section I

Mr. Gonzalez is shown recovering in a hospital room. A physiotherapist comes twice everyday to exercise the limbs. Mrs Gonzalez is seated in a chair next to Mr. Gonzalez.

Physiotherapist *(while exercising the limbs.)*: You have made very good recovery Mr. Gonzalez. Soon you would be able to do your daily chores.

Mr. Gonzalez: It's the result of your efforts.

Mrs. Gonzalez: Doctors have told us that physiotherapy exercises was the only effective treatment. Mr. Gonzalez is getting discharged from the hospital today. You'll have to come to our house for his physiotherapy.

Physiotherapist: Iam on regular duties at the hospital. I shall ask some colleague who stays near your house to attend to Mr. Gonzalez. I'll give you his address after talking to him. By now you too must have learnt the exercises.

Mrs. Gonzalez: Yes.

Physiotherapist: Ok. I'll take leave for today.

Mrs. Gonzalez: Ok. Thank you.

(Physiotherapist leaves the ICU.)

Mrs. Gonzalez: Robert, How are you?

Mr. Gonzalez: Much better Annie.

Mrs. Gonzalez: The grandchildren are coming to see you. Its almost 35 days in the hospital. Today you shall be discharged. John has started walking properly. Simmy taught him.

(Mr. Gonzalez Smiles.)

Soon Michael, Elizabeth, Simmy and John enter the room. Michael is holding Johns hand. John has started walking properly.

Simmy runs to grandpa and holds his hand. Grandpa hugs his granddaughter.

Soon John comes closer to the bed walking. Grandpa hugs John as well.

Simmy: How are you grandpa?

Mr. Gonzalez: I am fine children.

John: How....r..you?

Mr. Gonzalez: John has learnt to walk and to talk better.

John: Grandpa, grandpa I can.... walk..Grand pa come walk.

Pulls grandpa. Grandpa tries to walk with John.

John: Grandpa ..... walk....walk....

Everyone smiles.

John: Come grandpa, walk.

Mr. Gonzalez: *(takes a chair and John in his arms)* John, soon we shall be at our home. We shall walk together.

Everyone smiles.

Dr. Prakash enters the room with few doctors.

Dr Prakash: Mr. Gonzalez, How are You?

Mr. Gonzalez: Fine Doctor. Fit as before.

Dr Prakash: Mr. Gonzalez ,we are discharging you from the hospital. I have written all the medicines that you have to continue. Physiotherapy has to be performed on a regular basis.

Mr. Gonzalez: Doctor I have talked to the physiotherapist from the hospital. He shall be giving us the address of his colleague. He has promised that his colleague shall come daily to the house for physiotherapy exercises.

Dr Prakash: Good. All the best Mr. Gonzalez.

Mr. Gonzalez: Thank you doctor.

Dr. Prakash leaves the room.

Simmy: Grandpa tell us a story.

Elizabeth: Simmy, when grandpa returns home he shall tell you stories.

Mr. Gonzalez: Let me tell them a short story.

Ok, John and Simmy, I shall tell you a short story.The title of the story is Health and Nutrition.

Health and Nutrition

Health and nutrition were born in same village and shared the same birth day. Health and nutrition lived a cheerful and happy life. Health was robust and nutrition was of the light built. Apart from studying at school, health and nutrition used to exercise daily and work with their parents. After completing their studies health and nutrition took up jobs in the nearby city. The city life was fast and busy.

Excessive industrialization had changed the environment. The work was sedentary and involved very little exercises. During their stay in the city health and nutrition established many new acquaintances. Among them was a workmate named obesity. Obesity took health and nutrition to many fast food restaurants. Health and nutrition started taking fatty food in excess. Both became obese too and a fateful day Health had to be hospitalized. The doctor advised health to take light meals and fresh air. Health and nutrition followed the advice and were soon healthy as before.

Everyone smiles.

Simmy: You seem to have learnt new stories from the hospital. Short but nice story grandpa.

Mr. Gonzalez: I was told this story by a nurse who looked after me at the hospital. She used to tell me a lot of short stories everyday. I shall tell you more stories when I reach home.

Michael: Mother and father, I shall clear the bills before discharge.

Mrs. Gonzalez: Ok

Michael: Come Elizabeth.

Michael and Elizabeth leave the room

ACT 5
Section II

Mrs. Gonzalez was serving her husband day in and day out since he got admitted in the hospital. Mr. Gonzalez was in the room and about to be discharged, when Dr Diya enters the room.

Dr Diya: Hello, Mrs. Gonzalez how are you?

Mrs. Gonzalez: Fine and healthy.

Dr Diya: I have come to see your husband. Dr Prakash asked me to have a review.

Mrs. Gonzalez: He is much better now. Have a look.

Mr. Gonzalez: Hello Dr Diya. I am much better now.

Dr Diya examines Mr. Gonzalez. She looks at ECG and the treatment chart.

Dr Diya: Mrs. Gonzalez, your husband is perfect health wise. He can be discharged from the hospital.

Mrs. Gonzalez: Dr Prakash was also telling us the same. He is discharging the patient today itself.

Dr Diya: Good. I have written few drugs which he shall have to continue even after discharge.The drugs shall be mentioned in the discharge summary.

Mrs. Gonzalez: Thank you Dr Diya. (Dr Diya is about to leave. Mrs. Gonzale stops her near the door)

Dr Diya I wanted to have one more consultation from you before leaving the hospital. Can I take an appointment?

Dr Diya: What happened? I have already given you

the medicines. Continue taking the medicines.

Mrs. Gonzalez: Just a routine check-up before the discharge.

Dr Diya: Why not? Come anytime between morning 8 to evening 5.

Mrs. Gonzalez: Dr Diya, thank you, I shall come today itself before the discharge.

Mr. Gonzalez: Dr Diya thank you for all the help you have given.

Dr Diya: Do not mention. Its our duty.

Dr Diya: Ok I shall take leave now. I have some patients in the ward to see.

Dr Diya leaves the room.

Dr Grover enters the room.

Mr. Gonzalez and Mrs. Gonzalez: Hello, Dr Grover.

Dr Grover: Hello. I was told that you are getting discharged. Dr Prakash asked me have a review before the discharge. You look in such a perfect shape. I will have a look at the CT.

He takes a CT and haves a good look.

Dr Grover: Yes the swelling is much reduced. Good you can be discharged.

Mr. Gonzalez: Thank you doctor.

Dr Grover: Need not thank us. Thank Dr Prakash. Ok I shall leave. All the best.

Dr Grover leaves the ward.

Soon a trolley arrives in the room with two ward boys.

Ward Boy: Mr. Gonzalez we are shifting you to the ambulance which shall drop you to your residence.

Mr. Gonzalez: Ok

The ward boys transfer Mr. Gonzalez on the trolley and shift him to the ambulance.

Mrs. Gonzalez also leaves the room with Mr. Gonzalez.

ACT 6

Dr. Diya resting on a sofa at her house. She is sipping juice kept in a glass. Another glass is kept on the table. The room is well decorated and furnished.

The door bell rings.

Dr. Diya opens the door. Dr Prakash at the door.

Dr. Diya: What took you so long?

Dr. Prakash: I was busy discharging a patient Mr. Gonzalez.

Dr. Diya: The same patient on bed no. 6 in neurology ward?.

Dr. Prakash: Yes.

Dr. Diya: His wife also got discharged today.

Dr. Prakash: Discharged? When was she admitted for anything?

Dr. Diya: She had mild chest pain a few days back. It was good that she was in the hospital and got immediate treatment. She came for another consultation today. I told her that she was fine and should continue the medicines.

She recovered well. She served her husband so well. She asked me not to tell anything about her condition to her husband till he recovered completly. I was happy that the couple was so much in love. Her care and devotion to her husband contributed to her husbands recovery.

Dr Prakash: True. Doctors can work according to the science of their times, but the well wishes of the attenders also contribute to the recovery, at least psychologically.

Dr. Diya: Well said.

Dr. Prakash: She was with the patient all the while and didn't her son came to know about her illness?

Dr. Diya: She sent her son and the other members of the family on tour to some hill station after Mr. Gonzalez was shifted to the ward and was recovering well. It was during this period she was admitted to cardiac care ward for few hours of observation.

Dr. Prakash: She turned out to be a very dedicated and strong woman.

Dr. Diya: Yes. She was with her husband during the entire treatment. She used to tell me about how both she and her husband had met at the same hill station and how both had proposed to each other. It was a romantic tale. She was smiling all the way.

Dr. Prakash: Good for the Gonzalez's family. If Mr Gonzalez had reported to the hospital within 3 hours he would have got discharged many days earlier.Do you Know that in neurology a patient must report within 3 hours to be treated properly with clot dissolving drugs for stroke?

Dr Diya: Yes, I have heard about the new clot dissolving drugs and the time period for reporting to the hospital.

Dr. Prakash: Enough about the patients. How are you? You are looking beautiful for the occasion.

Dr. Diya: Let us get ready for the party. Where are we going tonight?

Dr. Prakash: I have booked seats for both of us in your favorite restaurant.

Dr. Diya: Good. At least you remember the day.

Dr. Prakash: I Had to. Its only once in a year we celebrate our wedding anniversary. Like the Gonzalez couple we too have successfully completed 5 years of our marriage.

(Dr. Diya and Dr Prakash leave the room)

ICU-2

(A short play to present the treatment of a patient of stroke in ICU when he arrives on time....)

ICU-2

ICU-2 has a similar story as the ICU –1. ICU –1 presented to us the different treatment options in a patient of stroke. ICU –2 presents

the same situation at Mr. Grover's house. The difference is the treatment offered to a patient of stroke when the patient reaches within 3 hours.

Characters:

Rakesh: Rakesh is the central character. His family resides in a rented house. He works in a factory nearby his house and also has a small shop in the market nearby which he opens during the evening.

Sheela: Wife of Rakesh. A housewife. A caring and loving nature.

Subhesh Grover: Son of Grover family. A college student. Is learning to be responsible.

Rani: Daughter of Grover Family. A commerce student in the same college as Subhesh.

Dr Sudheer: An ICU resident at the City hospital.

Dr Prakash: A Neurologist at the City Hospital

Mr Pandey: An office colleague of Rakesh.

ACT 1

At the rented residence of Mr. Rakesh Grover. Its located in the same colony as Mr. Gonzalez. The house is simple and clean. The door opens into the entrance room which has few sofas and a round table. A kitchen door opens on the right. A dining table kept near the kitchen door. Two doors on the left for two rooms. The door bell rings. Sheela opens the door. Rakesh returns from his office with a bag in his hand. Rakesh keeps the bag on the sofa and leans over the sofa.

Sheela: I'll get some water for you...

Sheela gets a glass of water from the kitchen.

Rakesh takes the glass.

Sheela: Is everything ok? You look very tired. I'll get some juice for you.

Rakesh: Yes,a glass of juice would be very refreshing.

Sheela goes to the kitchen again, prepares a fresh glass of juice and returns to the entrance hall.

Sheela: Here take some juice and you shall be fine again.

(Rakesh takes sips from the glass)

Rakesh: I have filled the forms of the new housing scheme, I was talking to you about. The results of the scheme shall be declared after a lucky draw on the computer.

Sheela: Good. We have to settle somewhere before

the retirement. The children too were anxious. How long can we stay in a rented house? Where did you take the money from?

Rakesh: I took it from the provident fund.

Sheela: If it was not so necessary, I would have insisted on keeping the provident fund safe for the future.

Rakesh:Yes it was necessary. You know how difficult it is to live in a city without a proper accommodation. For years we have lived in a rented residence. My factory job is only for two more years.

Sheela: Do you want something to eat?

Rakesh: Not yet. I shall take a proper bath before lunch. Let the children come from their college.

We shall have lunch together.

Rakesh goes to the bathroom.

Sheela goes to the kitchen to prepare the lunch.

Soon Rakesh comes out of the bathroom looking more fresh.

Rakesh: The children have not returned home from their college yet?

Sheela: Not yet. They shall be coming soon. I'll keep the lunch on the table.

Rakesh goes to the room

There is a knock-on the door Sheela opens the door.

Subhesh and Rani enter the entrance room.

Subhesh and Rani go to their room one by one and come out with their dresses changed.

Subhesh: Mother is the lunch ready?

Sheela: Yes I have kept it ready in the kitchen. Rani come and bring the lunch to the dining table.

Rani: Ok, mother.

Rani brings lunch from the kitchen and keeps it on the dining table.

Subhesh and Rani go to the bathroom one by one and come out with their hands and faces washed. They take their seat on the table.

Sheela: Rakesh come and take your lunch.

Rakesh takes his seat on the table.

Sheela serves everyone their lunch. All the four people start eating their lunch.

Sheela: Your father has filled the application of the new housing scheme.

Subhesh: Good. We do require a place of our own. Myself and Rani have to still share a room.

Rani: These housing schemes. It is much better to purchase a house on ones own.

Rakesh: If we don't get a house in the housing scheme, we shall buy a house on our own.

Subhesh: If you had listened to me, we would have lived in our own house a few years back. We delayed buying a house in a colony in which a friend of mine has taken a flat for a very low price. Just a delay of few days and the rates of the flats were doubled.

Everyone finishes off their lunch.

Sheela brings a plate full of fruits and keeps the fruits on the table.

Everyone takes a fruit of their choice.

Rani: Mother our college is organizing a picnic next month. Each of us have to contribute some money.

Sheela: You were saving some money for the picnic trip. By now you must have collected sufficient enough.

Rani: I have saved enough pocket money. I only require your permission for the picnic.

Sheela: You can go to the picnic if you want.

Subhesh: I also want to join the coaching classes next month.

Rakesh: Give us all the details about the coaching classes, then only I can give you the permission.

Subhesh: Ok I shall get all the details.

Sheela: Rakesh come to the room, and take some rest.

Rakesh: Coming. Children you also take some rest.

Rani: I have to study for my exams, I shall be in the entrance hall.

Everyone goes to their rooms. Rani brings some books and stays in the entrance hall and prepares for her exams.

ACT 2

Next morning Mrs. Sheela wakes up first in the house.She goes to the kitchen and prepares tea.Soon other members of the family are also awake. They finish off their morning rituals and take their tea. They also start preparing themselves for their colleges and offices. Mrs. Sheela is busy preparing breakfast in the kitchen.

Subhesh: Mother where have you kept my jeans.

Sheela: *(from the kitchen)* Its in the suitcase.

Rani: Mother when are you going to comb my hairs?

Sheela: I am preparing breakfast. I'll come as soon as the breakfast is ready.

Rakesh: Sheela where have you kept those headache tablets which Dr Diwakar had prescribed a few days back? *(Sheela comes to entrance hall from kitchen)*

Sheela: Why do you require headache tablets? Better take an appointment with Dr Diwakar.

Rakesh: I am having slight headache since yesterday night.I shall take an appointment with Dr Diwakar in the evening.

Sheela: You should get examined properly. Do You know about Mr. Gonzalez who stays few houses away?

Rakesh: Yes, Yes I do know about him.He is still hospitalized.

I went to the hospital yesterday.He looked much better now. He shall be shifted to the ward in few days.

Sheela: He also had slight headache and landed up in the hospital.

(Sheela gets few tablets)

Rakesh takes the tablets.

Sheela goes to Rani's room and combs her hair. Soon she comes out of the room and washes her hands and goes to the kitchen.

Sheela: Everyone come for the breakfast.

Subhesh and Rani come out of their rooms fully prepared for the college.

They take their seat at the table. Rakesh also takes his seat.

Sheela serves each of them their breakfast from the kitchen.

Sheela: Rakesh, take leave if you are not all right.

Rakesh: I have some important work at the office today so I can't take a leave. I shall return home as soon as the work is over.

Subhesh: Father take care of your health too. You have not taken any leave for the entire year.At least take leave on such a day.

Rakesh: I shall take an appointment from doctor. Diwakar in the evening. So don't worry.

Everyone finish their breakfast.

Subhesh and Rani: Ok mother and father, we are leaving for the college.

Sheela: There is some juice for you both in the

kitchen. Take before going to the college.

Subhash goes to the kitchen and brings two glasses of juice. He gives one to Rani. They both finish drinking the juice and leave for the college.

Sheela: Do you insist on going to the office. Better take some rest.

Rakesh: I shall be fine.

Sheela: As soon as the work is over, return home.

Rakesh: ok.

Rakesh leaves for the office.

Sheela takes her breakfast.

She takes a small book, leans over the sofa and starts reading.

Sheela is reading her book when the phone bell rings.

Sheela picks the phone.

Sheela: Hello Sheela speaking.....Hello Mr. Pandey how are you?.....What happened?....Mr. Grover admitted to the City Hospital ....

Yes he had slight headache in the morning. He took some tablets ....Weakness of the left arm... I shall be coming to the hospital soon.

Sheela calls up her son at the college.

Sheela: Hello Subhesh Grover on line....come

soon to the City Hospital. Your father is admitted there.....He is admitted with weakness of the left arm..... Mr. Pandey called from the office.... Ok come soon.....Don't Call Rani, she is having her exams today. We shall tell her in the evening.... Don't delay.

Sheela goes to her room and comes out in different dress. She soon leaves the room.

ACT 3

At the hospital, same ICU as in Play ICU-1. Mr Rakesh on a bed in the ICU. Few IV lines and IV fluids on flow. A nurse near each patient. Mr. Pandey and a colleague seated on two chairs in front of the resident doctor *(Dr Sudheer)* table and chair.

Dr. Sudheer introduces himself and asks Mr. Pandey and his colleague their names.

Dr Sudheer: Kindly give me details about what happened?

Mr. Pandey: Mr. Rakesh was at the office when he suddenly became drowsy in his chair at around 1 pm. He also had numbness and left hand weakness. According to his wife, he had slight headache in the afternoon yesterday.He took some headache tablets. The office people shifted him immediately to the hospital.

Resident: Did he have any fits on the way?

Mr. Pandey: No.

Resident: Does he have any sugar or BP?

Mrs. Gonzalez: Only his wife shall be able to tell. I called her and told her about his condition. She shall be coming soon.

We are his office mates and do not know much about his medical background.

Dr Sudheer: Okay. Dr. Prakash shall be here any moment. He shall examine Mr. Rakesh and shall talk to both of you. We have got his CT done and the CT doesn't show any bleeding. Since the patient has weakness of the left arm, it looks like a stroke. Dr Prakash might advice a clot dissolving medicine for the patient because the patient has arrived within 3 hours to the hospital. Since the medicine has to be given urgently hence kindly give your consent for the treatment and sign these papers.The medicine carries a slight risk of bleeding.

Mr. Pandey: Doctor give him the best possible medicine.I shall sign the papers. Doctor I have a question to ask. How come the patient has a stroke when the CT is normal?

Dr Sudheer: The CT scan of a patient is usually normal in early stroke. Only after 2-3 days the CT shows some finding.

Only a MRI detects early stroke.In an emergency we often rely on clinical findings and no signs of bleeding in CT to detect a stroke without getting an MRI. An MRI takes more than 30 minutes and the initial few hours are critical for giving the clot dissolving medicines like TPA.

(Mr. Pandey signs the papers)

Dr. Sudheer: Send Mrs. Rakesh to ICU as soon as she arrives. *(to the Nurse)*

Sister note the phone numbers of the patient and his attenders.

Complete other formalities as well. Get me the treatment chart. I shall start the patient on some medicines. Dr Prakash shall be here soon and decide the rest of the treatment.

Mr. Pandey writes the phone number and address.

Mr. Pandey: Doctor call us if there is any requirement.

Mr. Pandey and his colleague leave ICU.

Dr Prakash *(Neurologist)* enters the ICU.

Dr Prakash: Where is the new patient Mr.Rakesh.

Resident: On bed no 4.*(Both doctors walk to bed no. 4)*

The resident takes Dr. Prakash to Mr. Rakesh and presents the relevant medical history.

Resident: Mr. Rakesh is a 52 years old male. Presented with headache since yesterday afternoon. Took some headache tablets. Was at the office when he became drowsy. Had numbness in left arm followed by left arm weakness at 1 pm. Was shifted to the hospital immediately. On examination..

Dr Prakash: Dr Sudheer let me examine the patient on my own. Mr. Rakesh I am Dr Prakash. I shall be treating you. How are you?

Mr. Rakesh: *(drowsily)* ....Fine ....

Dr Prakash examines Mr. Rakesh.

Dr. Prakash: Move your left arm Mr. Rakesh.

(tries to move his left arm. Dr Prakash notices the weakness.)

Dr Prakash: Show me the treatment chart. *(scribbles few drugs on the treatment chart.)* Start these medicines. Show me the CT.

Dr Sudheer shows the CT to Dr Prakash.

Dr Prakash: Ok. CT doesn't show any bleeding The patient has a stroke just like Mr. Gonzalez. Since the patient has arrived within 3 hours we shall give him the clot dissolving medicine. Have you taken any consent from the attendants for giving the medicine?

Dr Sudheer: Yes, I have taken consent from the office attendants for giving the drug. His wife shall be arriving at the hospital soon.

Dr Prakash: Prepare the patient for treatment with clot dissolving medicine –TPA. Stabilise the BP and get these tests done. I am writing the dose of the drug in the treatment chart. Call me up when everything is ready.

Dr Sudheer sends the lab tests and the samples. Dr Prakash leaves the ICU. Soon the tests results are available. A ward boy brings the lab reports. Dr. Sudheer reads the reports.

Dr Sudheer is about to call Dr Prakash when Dr. Prakash enters the ICU again.

Dr Prakash: Is everything ready?

Dr Sudheer: Yes, The patient's BP is normal and other tests are also normal.

Dr Prakash reads the test report.

Dr Prakash: Ok. Give the clot dissolving drug as written in the treatment chart. Mr.Rakesh we are giving you a medicine. Keep telling us about your condition.

Mr. Rakesh: Ok.

The nurse gives the drug as per the treatment chart.

After a while.

Mr. Rakesh: *(happily)* Doctor Prakash look the

weakness has improved.

Mr. Rakesh moves the hand properly.

Dr Prakash: Congrats, Mr. Rakesh.

Mr. Rakesh: Thank you Doctor Prakash.Thank you Dr Sudheer.

Dr Prakash: Dr Sudheer keep the patient on continuous monitoring. Keep the BP within normal limits and get a CT done after 4 hours.

Dr Sudheer: Ok ,sir.

Dr Prakash leaves the ICU.

Dr Sudheer: *(to the nurse)* Measure the BP 1/2 hourly.

Nurse: Ok doctor.

Dr Sudheer begins examining the patients on other beds.

The phone bell rings. Dr Sudheer picks up the phone.

Dr Sudheer: Hello Mrs.Sheela ....You are the wife of Mr. Rakesh ....He has responded to the treatment well ......Yes you can come to see him.

Dr Sudheer keeps the phone.

Mrs. Sheela soon enters the ICU

Mrs. Sheela: *(To the nurse)* Where is Mr. Rakesh. He was admitted to the hospital in the afternoon.

Nurse: He is on bed number 4.

Mrs. Sheela: Yes I can see him.

(goes near the bed of Rakesh)

Mrs. Sheela: Dear Rakesh, what happened? How are you?

Rakesh: I am perfectly fine. I had sudden left arm weakness and numbness on the left leg. The doctors have given me the clot dissolving medicine. See my arm and leg are completely normal. (Rakesh moves both his left leg and arm) The office people shifted me to the hospital quickly. Mr.Pandey has been very helpful. He promptly called for the office ambulance.

Mrs. Sheela: Thanks to the creator of the universe. Thanks to all the doctors and thanks to your officemates for shifting you to the hospital. *(Sheela takes a chair next to the bed)*. Subhesh shall be coming to the hospital soon. You take rest, I'll talk to the doctor.

She calls the nurse and asks about the doctor.

Mrs.Sheela:Nurse, where is the doctor?

Nurse: You can talk to the duty doctor Dr Sudheer at present. He is seated on the chair.

Sheela *(goes near the chair)*: Dr Sudheer how is Mr. Rakesh Grover?

Dr Sudheer: Mrs. Sheela, Please take a seat.

Sheela takes a chair kept nearby.

Dr Sudheer: Today morning Mr. Rakesh came to the Hospital with sudden onset of left arm weaknes.Since he arrived in the hospital within 3 hours we gave him a clot dissolving medicine. He improved within few minutes.

Presently his condition is very stable. He shall be shifted to the ward in the morning and discharged from the hospital in the next few days.

Subhesh enters the ICU.

Subhesh: Mother where is father? How is he?

Sheela: He is fine.The doctors have given him the clot dissolving medicine and he has improved almost completely. He is on bed no 4.

Subhesh: *(goes to bed no 4 and talks to his father)* How are you father?

Rakesh: Much better. I have improved completely. Subhesh *(holds his father's hands)*

Subhesh: *(returns to Dr Sudheer)* Dr Sudheer, how is father?

Dr Sudheer: He is perfectly healthy. Tomorrow he shall be shifted to the ward. Dr Prakash shall be here soon. He shall talk to both of you and tell you more about the patient.

Dr Prakash enters the ICU.

Dr Prakash: Hello, you both must be with the new patient Mr. Rakesh?

Mrs. Sheela: Yes.

Dr Prakash: Hello I am Dr Prakash. Your patient has responded very well to the therapy. He came with left arm weakness which has shown very good improvement.His office people were very helpful.They brought him to the hospital at the right time.

Mrs. Sheela: Dr Sudheer told us everything about it. We are grateful for the treatment to all the doctors.

Dr Prakash: Doctors act only according to the science of their generation.They can't do anything more.You must thank only the office people who brought him at the right time.

Mrs. Sheela: The office people shall be thanked too.

Dr Prakash: Ok Mrs. Grover all the best. The patient shall be shifted to the ward in the morning. I shall come again to the ward in the morning.

Sheela and Subhesh: Thank you once again doctor.

Dr Prakash leaves the ICU.

Dr Sudheer: You both can arrange a room coming morning.

Mrs. Sheela: Thank you, Dr. Sudheer.

(Sheela & Subhesh leave the ICU.)

ACT 4

Mr. Rakesh is soon discharged from the hospital. On the day when Rakesh returns home the entire family is seated on the dining table to have their lunch. Sheela has prepared special lunch for everyone.

Rakesh: You have prepared my favourite dishes today. I am very happy to be back home.

Rani: Mother prepared them all. She was busy since today morning.She has prepared dishes using minimal oil and fats. The dietician at the hospital advised her to do so.

Sheela: Rakesh you must thank life for granting you health.

I must thank Mr. Pandey for being so helpful. The doctors told me that he brought you to the hospital immediately due to which they could treat you properly.

Rakesh: Yes, Pandey was very helpful. We must invite him and his family for lunch tomorrow.

Subhesh: Father, is the drug so effective?

Rakesh: When Pandey took me to the hospital I had left arm weakness like Mr. Gonzalez. The weakness improved within few minutes, once the drug was given.

Sheela: Medical science has made good advancement then.

Rakesh: I wasn't expecting such dramatic recovery then. As soon as I was admitted doctors got a CT scan of the brain, stabilized the BP, got few lab tests and gave the clot dissolving medicine.

Sheela: Science keeps changing with the times with every new discovery and invention. We couldn't have expected such treatment few years back.

Rakesh: Science shall keep evolving with the times. We can still expect more discoveries and more inventions.

Sheela: You have to continue taking few medicines. So don't be careless. Take rest for a week.

Rakesh: I think I should join the office as soon as possible. I have plenty of work at the office.

Sheela: Take a few more days rest. I have already told the office people.You shall be granted holiday for another week.

Rakesh: I have already taken 1 week's holiday. I must join the office tomorrow.

Sheela: You better agree to what I said.

Rakesh: Ok,Ok.

Rani: Mother I am very angry that you didn't tell me about father.

Sheela: You had your exams. I told Subhesh to do so.

Rani:Next time onwards don't do like this to me.

Sheela: How were your exams? Didn't ask you before due to your father's health.

Rani: All the exams were easy. I shall pass easily.

Subhesh and Rani finish their lunch and go to their room. Rakesh is about to return to his room when there is a knock at the door. Sheela opens the door.

Mr. Pandey enters the entrance hall. Rakesh and Mr. Pandey wish each other and are seated on the sofas of the entrance hall.

Mr Pandey: I was returning from the office when few officemates told us that Rakesh has returned home.How are you?

Rakesh: Completely fit and healthy. I am grateful to all the office people for transferring me to the hospital within the critical period. I am specifically grateful to you for being so helpful.

Mr. Pandey:Don't thank me so much. I just arranged an ambulance.

Sheela: Your entire family are invited for lunch tomorrow and you can't refuse to come.

Mr. Pandey:Ok, Ok. My wife also wanted to see Rakesh so both of us shall come for the lunch tomorrow.

Sheela: The entire family.

Mr. Pandey: Ok.

Rakesh: How is everyone at the office? I want to rejoin tomorrow itself but Sheela insists on a week's rest.

Mr. Pandey: Better take some rest.

Sheela goes to kitchen and brings two glasses of juice.

Sheela gives one glass to Rakesh and another to Mr Pandey. Both finish drinking juice.

Mr Pandey: Ok Rakesh I shall take leave. I shall come for the lunch tomorrow at your house with my wife and two children.

Rakesh: Ok. See you at the lunch tomorrow.

Sheela: Namaskar Pandeyji.

Mr Pandey leaves the entrance hall.

Rakesh: When are the results of the housing scheme scheduled to open?

Sheela: The results must be out today.

Rakesh: Where is the paper?

Sheela brings the newspaper.

Rakesh searches for his number. Rakesh smiles...

POEM

The Creator and Creation (Sun)

The poem is part of collection of poems under the title "Creator and the creation" to be published soon. Nature's various aspects are written as poems.The poem "The Stream" published in previous book " Tenants and Handshake" is also from the same series. The poem "The creator and creation-The Sun" presents the importance of light emanating from a self illuminous source of light.

Self illuminous, shining with brilliance
Visible in the presence
The pathways of excellence
Such radiant is the light
One can see the world around
The roads which lead us
to our destination.
Witness to all the plays of the creation
And all the passing stages
A source of enlightment
Imparting knowledge to every generation.
Truth, beauty, and perfection
are the attributes
Towards harmony oneness and balance
The light contributes.
Ensuring growth and development of the civilization
Becoming a constant source of inspiration
Glorifying thus the creator and the creation.
